CEDAR POINT

CP 1870

CedarPoint®

established 1870

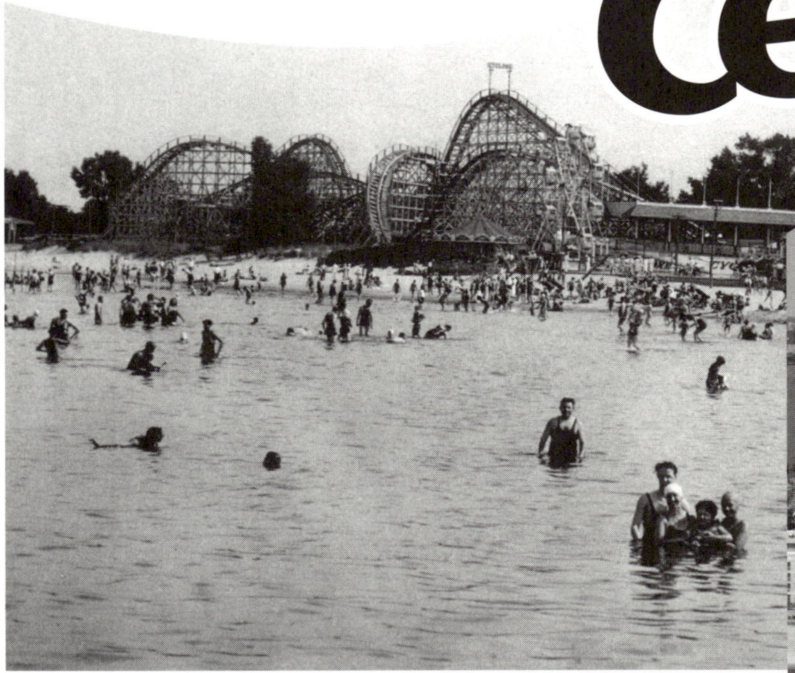

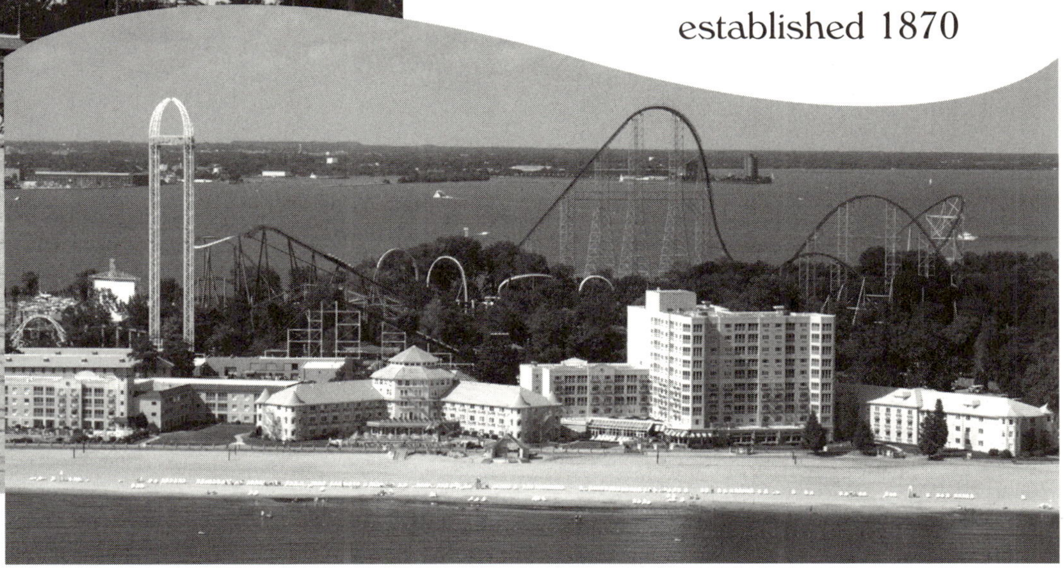

Proud to be part of Sandusky's history, and its future!

(419) 626-0830 • cedarpoint.com

John George Buderer settled from Germany to Sandusky in the early 1850's. The family's first business was a grocery and saloon located on the corner of Pearl and Sloan Streets, Sandusky. His grandson, Alvin George Buderer started his pharmacy career at the Sloan House Pharmacy (Bechberger and Kubach) in the 1920's. The pharmacy business was established in 1878. Today, John George's great grandson Jim and great-great grandson Matt own Buderer Drug on the corner of Hancock and Monroe, Sandusky.

In today's healthcare marketplace, diversity and innovation are the foundation of longevity. Some things stand the test of time.

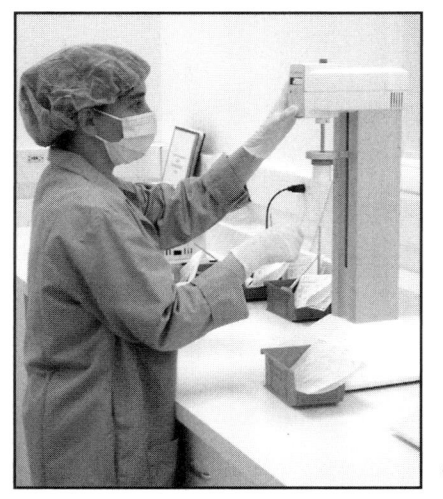
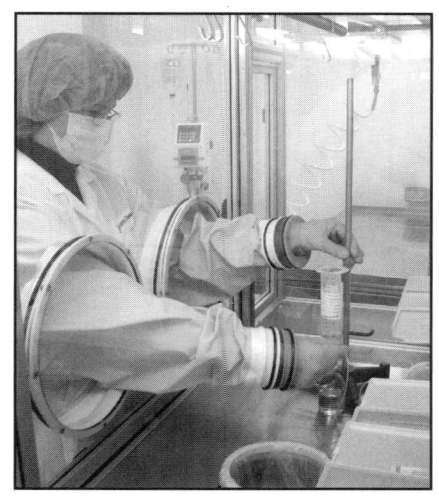

Buderer Drug Co.

Since 1878

A Compounding Pharmacy

Working together with patient and healthcare provider to meet each individual's specific medication needs.

633 Hancock St. • Sandusky • 419-627-2800 • www.budererdrug.com

A Pictorial History of the Early Years

ERIE COUNTY
&
THE ERIE ISLES

PRESENTED BY THE SANDUSKY REGISTER AND THE SANDUSKY LIBRARY

ACKNOWLEDGMENTS

We wish to thank the Milan Historical Museum and Huron Historical Society for their contributions to the book, as well as the hundreds of community members who came forward with historical photographs from family collections. This book would not have been possible without the tireless efforts of Sandusky Library's Ron Davidson, archives librarian, and Maggie Marconi, museum curator, who helped to select and organize the photographs, and Lori Schrader, public relations specialist, for administrative assistance. Finally, many thanks to the Sandusky Library Board of Directors, past and present, whose policies, since the beginning of the library's historical department in 1901, have ensured these important historic documents are collected and preserved for the community.

This book has been produced as a combined project of the *Sandusky Register* and the Sandusky Library.

Copyright© 2006 • ISBN: 1-59725-061-9

All rights reserved. No part of this book may be reproduced, stored in a retrieval system or transmitted in any form or by any means, electronic, mechanical, photocopying, recording or otherwise, without prior written permission of the copyright owner or the publisher.
Published by Pediment Publishing, a division of The Pediment Group, Inc. www.pediment.com Printed in Canada

Table of Contents

Foreword 4

Scenes 5

Commerce 12

Industry 35

Transportation 50

Lake Erie & The Isles 69

Sports & Leisure 79

Events 90

Public Service 99

Education 105

Society 116

Community 123

Foreword

For anyone who has ever tried to map a region's future, a trip through the past is usually a good place to start.

After all, those who don't remember their history are doomed to repeat it, or so the old saying goes.

And this region seems poised on the brink of change, from the jobs that power our economic engine to the schools that serve as the cornerstones of our communities.

The photographs on the following pages tell the story of the early years of Erie County and the islands of Lake Erie, a collection of memories of the people on whose shoulders we now stand and the events which shaped their lives and which, to a great degree, have shaped the region as we know it.

In the book's first pages, you'll encounter streetscapes and parkland, some of which we still enjoy today, others nothing more than memories. The next two sections will offer a look at the businesses and people that powered the region's early economy.

You'll see the businesses and people that once drove the economy and how those people spent their spare time — and the outfits they wore doing it.

We are grateful for the depth and vision of these early photographers, through the images they left behind. Their unflinching portrait of the early days of the region allows us to revisit these days as often as we wish, as long as we wish.

SCENES

Erie County, Ohio, can trace its heritage to the Revolutionary War, when numerous Connecticut residents were burned out of their homes by the raiding British. To compensate these citizens, who became known as the "sufferers," for their losses, the Connecticut Assembly awarded them 500,000 acres in the western-most portion of the Western Reserve, including Erie and Huron counties, which came to be known as The Firelands.

The Lake Erie Islands, although not actually part of the Firelands, are easily accessible from the shores of Lake Erie, and records of travel from the mainland to the islands date back to the 1800s.

The following pages show views of Erie County landmarks that still exist today, along with images that have long since disappeared from the landscape. Modes of transportation and of dress from another era are reflected in this section as citizens were photographed at work and at play.

Looking south from the Columbus Avenue slip, circa 1910. *Courtesy of Sandusky Library*

SCENES

An 1852 lithograph of Sandusky and the harbor published in *Gleason's Pictorial Drawing Room Companion* when Sandusky had 6,000 inhabitants, "with numerous docks, public buildings and numberless craft coming and going." *Courtesy of Sandusky Library*

Basin area, Milan, circa 1890, with embankment, levee, mills across the river, and the last basin warehouse and weigh/saleshouse. *Courtesy of Milan Historical Museum*

North side of the square in Milan, 1855. During harvest season, farmers' wagons would fill the square. *Courtesy of Milan Historical Museum*

Looking west from Wayne Street at East Washington Park, circa 1890. *Courtesy of Sandusky Library*

Main Street, Berlin Heights, 1896. Bechberger Drug Store is behind the first power pole. *Courtesy of Katharine Schneider*

A winter day on Main Street, Huron, 1905. Main Street had become known as "The Great White Way" because of the electricity. *Courtesy of Huron Historical Society*

Main Street of Castalia, circa 1905. *Courtesy of Greg Marshall*

Huron River Valley at Milan, 1900. *Courtesy of Milan Historical Museum*

Looking at the Sandusky waterfront at the foot of Columbus Avenue, circa 1901. The steamships *R.B. Hayes*, *A. Wehrle*, and *Arrow* are in the background. The Terminal Inn on the left was built in 1903 and burned in 1904. *Courtesy of Sandusky Library*

Residences on South Street in Berlin Heights, circa 1900. *Courtesy of Audrey Harrison*

Looking toward the courthouse, 1909. On the right is the drug store of John H. Bechberger and Henry Henkelman in the Sloane House Hotel on the corner of Columbus Avenue and West Washington Row. *Courtesy of Katharine Schneider*

West side of Main Street, Huron, 1909. *Courtesy of Huron Historical Society*

North side of the Milan Square, 1915. The drug store on the corner is the oldest commercial building in Milan. *Courtesy of Milan Historical Museum*

East side of the Milan Square showing the Lockwood block, 1915. Note the Sandusky, Milan, & Norfolk interurban tracks in the street. *Courtesy of Milan Historical Museum*

"Boy with the Boot" in Washington Park, 1939. Voltaire Scott brought the statue to Sandusky in 1895. It stood in Scott's Park, at the foot of Wayne Street, until the tornado of 1924. *Courtesy of Sandusky Library*

Washington Park, looking at the corner of Wayne Street and Washington Row, 1927. *Courtesy of William H. Grahl*

Looking north on the 200 block of Columbus Avenue during Christmas, 1930. *Courtesy of Sandusky Library*

Columbus Avenue as seen from the dock looking off the bow of a ship, circa 1939. *Courtesy of Sandusky Library*

COMMERCE

Long before the days of one-stop shopping, customers visited the local meat market, pharmacy, hardware, and shoe stores in their individual neighborhoods. Photos of these shops reflect the unique nature of these establishments.

The B.R. Ward store, east of Huron, for example, boasts "bathing outfits" in their confectionery and grocery store. An abundance of produce is pictured in Riccelli's Grocery, a business that was also well-known for its roasted peanuts.

Cigar shops were common and saloons were popular gathering places. Dad's Lunch, Sandusky, remains etched in memory for its Limburger cheese sandwiches and pickled herring.

Proud shop owners, along with photos of their wares, employees and patrons, appear in the following pages. Note the images we aren't likely to see today: A hat-wearing donkey on the streets of Sandusky, for example, or a wide variety of merchandise available for 25 cents or less.

Schweinfurth Bros. store, West Park Street and Hayes Avenue, circa 1910. John, right, and Simon Schweinfurth are standing on either side of the front entrance. *Courtesy of Sandusky Library*

Sloane House Hotel, Columbus Avenue and West Washington Row. Rush Sloane, who served as a Sandusky mayor and was a noted abolitionist, opened the Sloane House Hotel in 1881. Thirty guest rooms with private baths were located on the third and fourth floor. The second floor was offices and the first floor was storefronts and the lobby. Nine years later he built the Sloane Block with storefronts on Washington Row. The J.H. Bechberger Drug Store was on the corner of the building. *Courtesy of Katharine Schneider.*

J&F Bock Barber Shop, 812 Water Street, 1886, was operated by Joseph and Frank Bock. *Courtesy of Sandusky Library*

John H. Bechberger in his first drug store in Berlin Heights, circa 1896. *Courtesy of Katharine Schneider*

Beecher House on West Washington Row with the Erie County Investment Company and Christian Science Reading Room upstairs, circa 1900. *Courtesy of Deborah Neese-Voltz*

Gathered in front of the interurban Waiting Room next to the Hotel Streck in Milan, circa 1900. *Courtesy of Sandusky Library*

John L. Rieger store sold boots and shoes, 602 Hancock Street, circa 1888. *Courtesy of Sandusky Library*

J.L. Bonn & Son, a grocery store on the northeast corner of Decatur and Adams streets, circa 1890. *Courtesy of Sandusky Library*

The C.F. Schumacher store sold boots, shoes, and rubbers, circa 1895. It was on the northeast corner of Hancock and Reese streets. *Courtesy of Sandusky Library*

A. Popke store sold men's clothing and dry goods, circa 1895. The store was at 712 Hancock Street in 1896 and 623 Hayes Avenue in 1898. *Courtesy of Sandusky Library*

J.G. Buderer, a grocery store at Pearl and Seneca streets, circa 1900. *Courtesy of Sandusky Library*

A. Smith Bakery at Tiffin Avenue and Pearl Street, circa 1900. *Courtesy of Sandusky Library*

The Huber Wolfe Hardware Co., October 19, 1909. *Courtesy of Audrey Harrison*

M.J. Bender & Co., a grocery store at Monroe and Hancock streets, 1904. *Courtesy of Sandusky Library*

COMMERCE

Koehler Bros. Meat Market at 529 E. Adams Street, 1890. Behind the case are owners John A. and Christopher Koehler. *Courtesy of Janice M. Ross*

Gathering in front of Hohler's Place, a Sandusky saloon at the northwest corner of Camp and Barker streets, circa 1905. *Courtesy of Sandusky Library*

Conrad Elbert, Jr., Pharmacy, 807 Columbus Avenue, circa 1910. *Courtesy of Sandusky Library*

Robrahn Tailoring Shop for ladies' clothing, 805 Market Street, circa 1910. Albert Robrahn is in the back. Clara Schaeffer Klemmt is on the right. *Courtesy of Sandusky Library*

Frank Riedy Cigar Store, 1027 Market Street, circa 1910. *Courtesy of Sandusky Library*

John Dietric Bremer and Marie Bremer standing on the steps of their grocery store on the southwest corner of Vine and Monroe streets, circa 1915. *Courtesy of Marlene Roberts*

West House Hotel was built in 1858 in time for the Ohio State Fair held in Sandusky that year. Built by brothers William T. West and Abel Kingsbury West on the corner of Columbus Avenue and Water Street, the West House Hotel had 250 rooms and a dining room that could seat 200-300 people. By 1888, the hotel featured an elevator, system of electric bells, steam heating, and electric lights. It was demolished in 1919. *Courtesy of Sandusky Library*

Nobil's Shoes and Rubbers, East Market Street, 1919. The building later housed Faroh's Candy. Standing, left to right: Henry Schmidt, Rocky Puckrin, unknown, Erma Smith, unknown, and Mr. Williams. *Courtesy of Janis Grathwol Burke*

Interior of Hotel Rieger, 1919. It was built in 1912 and opened with 60 rooms. *Courtesy of Roger Dickman*

Schade Theatre, 207-209 W. Market Street, 1918. The featured films included "My Four Years in Germany" and "The Reason Why." *Courtesy of Robert and Karen Deitz*

B.R. Ward store at Mitiwanga located along Ohio 2 and U.S. 6 between Huron and Vermilion, circa 1919. *Courtesy of Roger Dickman*

Interior of the Star Theater, a silent movie theater, looking toward the screen from the rear of the theater, circa 1920. The theater was on the east side of Columbus Avenue and was built in 1914 on the site of the Eleutheros Cooke house, the first stone house in Sandusky. The south wall of the theater was the original wall of the Cooke house. *Courtesy of Roger Dickman*

Storefront of Edward J. Windisch's drug store, 811 Hayes Avenue, circa 1920. *Courtesy of Roger Dickman*

Schweinfurth Bros. Grocery, 809 Hayes Avenue in Sandusky, circa 1920. *Courtesy of Sandusky Library*

George H. Speir's meat market, 1302 Camp Street, circa 1920. The second man from the right is Chester Scheufler. *Courtesy of Sandusky Library*

Acme Barber Shop at 116 Columbus Avenue, 1922. *Courtesy of Sandusky Library*

Perry & Bretz, a men's clothing store, 136 E. Market Street, circa 1925. *Courtesy of Sandusky Library*

Kingsbury Block, Columbus Avenue and East Washington Row, December 30, 1922. Demolition had begun on approximately 38 feet of the south end of the building by Commercial National bank to build a new bank on the site. The Kingsbury Block was built in 1894. A variety of businesses and offices occupied the building, including City Hall from 1913-1916 on the third floor. *Courtesy of Sandusky Library*

The new Commercial Bank was nearing completion, October 5, 1923. The building was at Columbus Avenue and East Washington Row and was built after approximately 38 feet of the 1894 Kingsbury Block was demolished. The bank failed during the Depression and was sold to the S.S. Kresge Co. Beginning in 1932, the H&S Bakery used the building. *Courtesy of Sandusky Library*

Dad's Lunch was in the 100 block of West Water Street, circa 1925. August J. Werner, standing behind the bar, owned the business that was known for its unique Limburger cheese sandwiches and pickled herring. Mr. Werner was a personal bartender for G.A. Boeckling, who helped the business that operated from the early 1920s through the mid-1930s. *Courtesy of Bill Werner*

Mr. Ruggiero Riccelli, left, and Felice "Phillip" Mariotti in Riccelli's Grocery on East Market Street, circa 1925. The store was well-known for its fruits and vegetables as well as its roasted peanuts. *Courtesy of Anna Fantozzi*

Looking into the Riccelli store at 119 E. Market Street, circa 1930. *Courtesy of Sandusky Library*

Newspaper carriers in front of the Citizens Banking Company, 160-170 E. Market Street, 1926. *Courtesy of Sandusky Library*

Sale at the Henry J. Close shoe store, 160 Columbus Avenue, after the death of Mr. Close, May 1926. Bamberger's Millinery Store is on the right.
Courtesy of Sandusky Library

The Wilcox Co., a dealer in dry goods, notions, and carpets at 139-145 Columbus Avenue, 1928. The Pelican Restaurant is on the left. *Courtesy of Sandusky Library*

McMahon's Barber Shop in the Hotel Rieger, 1925. *Courtesy of Sandusky Library*

A card advertising the Balcony, circa 1935. Originally called the Stadt Freiburg, an inn dating back to 1852, it was named the Balcony because of the famous men who had spoken from its balcony. At the time of the card, Otto J. Ketterer owned the business. *Courtesy of Arnold and Jean Mischler*

Dell Sartor on the steps of Miller Drug Co., Camp and Monroe streets, 1932. *Courtesy of Stephen J. Sartor*

F.W. Woolworth Co. employees, September 24, 1937. *Courtesy of Stephen J. Sartor*

Kresge Store on East Market Street. The store was destroyed by fire on March 31, 1939. *Courtesy of Sandusky Library*

INDUSTRY

"Largest fresh-water fish market in the world." "Ice capital of the Great Lakes."

Both honors distinguished the city of Sandusky in the late 1800s and early 1900s. Ice houses lined Sandusky Bay, with massive shipments of ice exported in as many as 40 or 50 insulated boxcars per day.

This industry, in conjunction with local wooden box and barrel-making, helped make the commercial fishing business boom for more than 100 years in the area.

Numerous vineyards and wineries dotted the landscape in this era as well, as vintners found the climate provided by Lake Erie conducive to the cultivation of grapes.

The Kelleys Island school district once hosted a significantly larger student population due to the sheer number of people who worked in the rapidly expanding grape-growing industry. Over the years, the number of vineyards dwindled, leaving only a handful to produce the region's wines today.

But in the early part of the century, many other area industries flourished, including agriculture, lumber, several breweries, a crayon company, dairy products, corrugated cardboard, limestone quarrying, and horseshoeing. A ball bat factory in Milan is featured in the following pages, as is the Michel Cooperage, which manufactured barrels.

Workers at the Bay View Foundry, circa 1910. Founded in 1908, the foundry was on McDonough Street between Market and Water streets. *Courtesy of Sandusky Library*

INDUSTRY

Moving ice for storage, circa 1875. Harvesting ice on Sandusky Bay was a major industry in Sandusky in the 19th century before refrigeration. *Courtesy of Sandusky Library*

Carriage & Wagon Works with an accompanying blacksmith shop, Tiffin Avenue by Washington Street, circa 1885. William Bing owned the business.
Courtesy of James A. Edwards

Mill at Venice, circa 1885. *Courtesy of Sandusky Library*

Weier Bros. Scrap Yard, 920 Franklin Street, circa 1890. The business was owned by John and Henry Weier. *Courtesy of Sandusky Library*

INDUSTRY

Schwehr Box Co., West Water and McDonough streets, made cigar boxes, circa 1880. *Courtesy of Sandusky Library*

Stang Brewery, 1885. Mr. Kuhman is on the left in the second row. Ida Stang is the girl in the center. *Courtesy of Mary Alice Appell*

Hinde & Dauch Paper Co. workers collecting straw for pulp, circa 1888. The company pioneered the process for making corrugated paper for boxes. *Courtesy of Sandusky Library*

Michel Bros. Cooperage works, East Market Street, 1890. *Courtesy of Janice M. Ross*

INDUSTRY

The M. Hommel Wine Co. cellar, circa 1895. *Courtesy of Karen and Robert Deitz*

The Consumers Ice Co. delivery wagon on West Washington Street, circa 1895. *Courtesy of Sandusky Library*

Milan ball bat factory in Milan, 1896. *Courtesy of Sandusky Library*

Wagons being manufactured by J.A. Loeffler for the J.M. Hastings Lumber Co., circa 1902. *Courtesy of Sandusky Library*

Scene in front of Sandusky Gas and Electric Co., circa 1900. *Courtesy of Robert and Karen Deitz*

INDUSTRY

Preparing ice for shipment, 1910. *Courtesy of Sandusky Library*

Harvesting ice on Sandusky Bay, December 1909. *Courtesy of Sandusky Library*

Prize won by William H. Taft, a barrel of sauerkraut, at the Elks fair in 1909. The barrel was manufactured by the Michel Bros. Cooperage Co. of Sandusky. *Courtesy of Sandusky Library*

Coles Livery, circa 1910. Standing, left to right: Ed Coles, Howard "Red" Wise, Adam Lieb, Dick Elmer, Harry Fletcher, and Willie Kleiger. Seated: George Guckert, Issac Coles, William Coles, Frank Townsend, and Jim Gilbert. In the front is Billie Coles. *Courtesy of Sandusky Library*

The last haul of the 1913 spring fishing season, July 3, 1913, from a postcard that reads: "Sandusky, the largest fresh-water fish market in the world." *Courtesy of Sandusky Library*

Martin's Ice Cream plant, circa 1915. *Courtesy of Sandusky Library*

INDUSTRY

Sandusky tractors made by the Dauch Manufacturing Co., 1917. The factory was at the foot of First Street. *Courtesy of John and Altina Schaeffer*

J.J. Thom Horse Shoeing and General Blacksmithing, circa 1920. The business was on Hayes Avenue near the underpass next to American Crayon Co. *Courtesy of Roger Dickman*

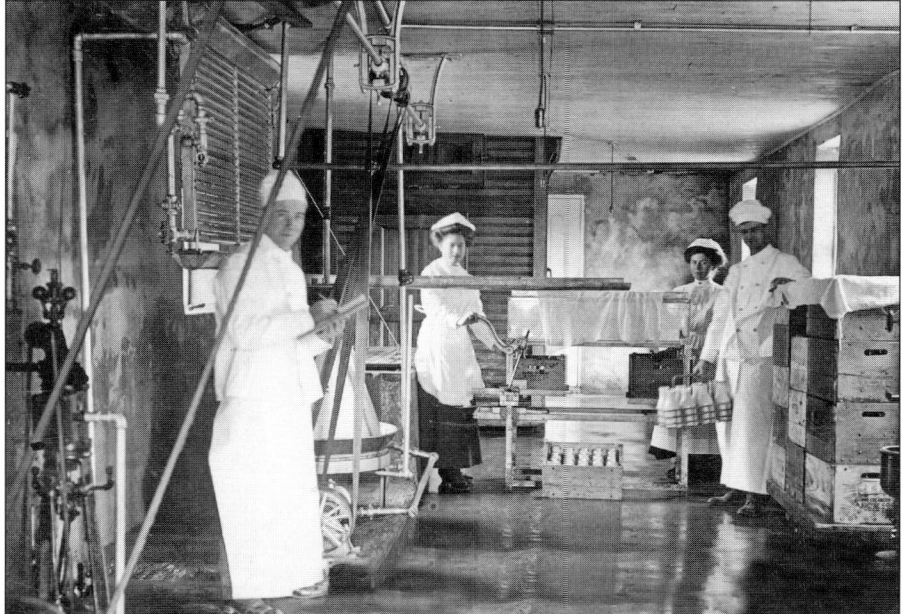

Interior of Esmond Dairy on Campbell Street, circa 1920. *Courtesy of Roger Dickman*

Matthews Engineering office, 607 King Street, April 23, 1923. *Courtesy of Sandusky Library*

Workers building the Sandusky coal docks, circa 1925. *Courtesy of Gary Kelley*

Delivery truck for The United Fisheries Co. on East Market Street, circa 1925. *Courtesy of Sandusky Library*

Wagner Quarry, 1926. *Courtesy of Sandusky Library*

The Consumers Ice & Fuel Co., 1329 First Street, 1927. *Courtesy of Sandusky Library*

INDUSTRY

Commercial fishing at Biemiller Cove, circa 1930. *Courtesy of Sandusky Library*

Post Fish Co. on Railroad Street between Wayne Street and Columbus Avenue, 1935. Standing third from the left is Fred Ohlemacher, born December 17, 1884, who worked for Post Fish for 34 years. *Courtesy of Marion Brownell Beese*

Threshing wheat on the Frank Balduff farm on Scheid Road west of Union Corners (U.S. 250 and Scheid Road), 1926. The crew is using a mechanical thresher and a 13-ton four-cylinder gasoline Altman-Taylor tractor. Earl Hart is driving the team, Lloyd Hart is on the straw stack, Rollie Scheid is in the grain box, Kenney Balduff is tending the blower, Louis Smith is tending the separator, Neil Hart is sitting on the separator, Harry Aust is pitching bundles into the feeder, Carl Bonningson is pitching bundles into the feeder, Frank Balduff is at the end of the feeder, Erwin Heuser is on the tractor, and the last person on the tractor is unidentified. *Courtesy of John and Alvina Schaeffer*

Schwab Cooperage and Supply Co., 317 Perry Street, August 1934. From the left, the eighth person is Mr. Schwab, the tenth is Ralph Ross, the eleventh is Ruth Rhonehouse, the twelfth is Paul Mielke, and the child is Janice Ross. *Courtesy of Janice M. Ross*

Working on the Patterson farm east of Huron off U.S. 6, circa 1930. *Courtesy of Becky Coleman*

Sandusky Daily News evening paper boys in front of the Daily News office on Water Street, 1936. Front row, left to right: Cliff Rabb, Don Strausser, John K. Schaefer, unknown, unknown, Robert Berardi, Robert Chambers, Don Gundlach, LeRoy Riedy, and Lynn Bickey. Second row: unknown, Jim McKenna, Dwight Hall, unknown, Junior Ebert, unknown, Bob Schlett, Don Albert, Carl Wilson, and Robert Nath. Back row: Harold Briest, unknown, unknown, Joe Schwartz, Lester Stimmel, John Strickfaden, unknown, Chuck Finley, Don Gentry, Charles Gentry, Milton Stimmel, Nelson Stimmel, and unknown. On the bicycles are Andy Kreimes, left, and unknown. *Courtesy of Don Gentry and Dr. John K. Schaefer*

Carp pens at Cold Creek in Venice, 1920. *Courtesy of Katharine Schneider*

Universal Clay Products, 1528 First Street, circa 1935. *Courtesy of Gary Kelley*

Esmond salt and ice refrigerated ice cream delivery truck, 1927. *Courtesy of Sandusky Library*

Apex Manufacturing Co. on First Street, circa 1940. June Ehrnsberger Neese is in the front row on the right and Geraldine Ehrnsberger Hoelzer, wearing a white blouse, is in the second row next to the conveyor. *Courtesy of Deborah Neese-Voltz*

TRANSPORTATION

Erie County and Lake Erie have historically offered excellent opportunities for the development of transportation by both land and water.

Photos represent the progress made through the decades, from horse and buggy to electric auto to convertible Cadillac. Horse-drawn streetcars preceded "interurbans," which were, in turn, abandoned as the popularity of automobiles increased and the state of the region's highways improved.

In 1835, General William Henry Harrison, not yet president, helped dedicate the first Ohio railroad at East Battery Park in Sandusky, marking what would prove to be a significant milestone in the history of the region — the establishment of railroads contributed greatly to the growth of Erie County.

Lake Erie, a natural source of transportation, has inspired progress in water travel over the years with steamboat travel to Cedar Point and the islands, followed by gasoline propeller boats and ferries.

Aviation has also played a role in our local history, with early airplanes built in Sandusky, aeroplanes and hyrdroplanes tested on Sandusky Bay and a record-setting over-the-water flight in 1910.

4-H club excursion to Kelleys Island on the Lake Shore Interurban shown on Columbus Avenue in Sandusky, September 12, 1931. The passengers were getting off the interurban to board the steamer *Chippewa* seen in the background. *Courtesy of Sandusky Library*

The first train in Milan on the W&LE Railroad, an excursion train arriving from Norwalk, 1877. Note the earthen platform and the flatcars carrying passengers. It was a 3-foot gauge rail line. *Courtesy of Milan Historical Museum*

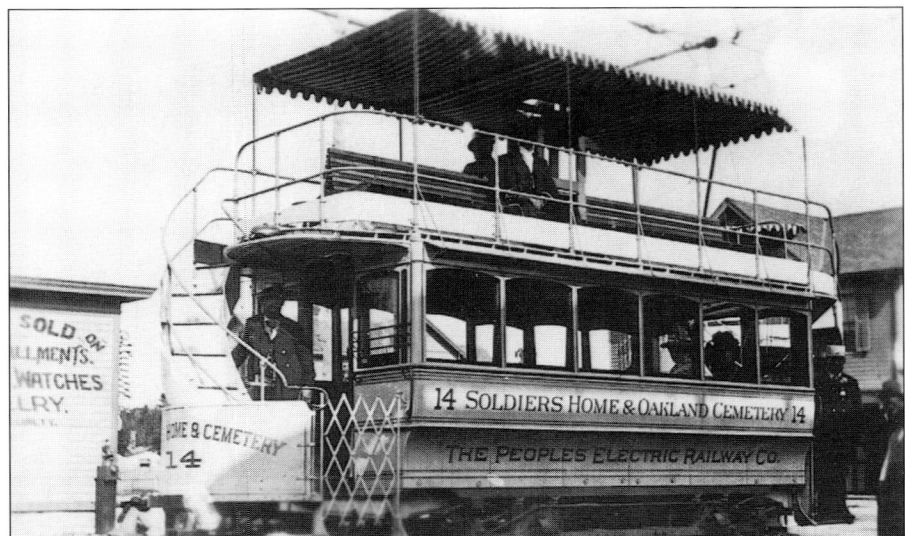

First Sandusky streetcar line, People's Electric Railway Company, 1892. Number 14 car served the Soldiers' and Sailors' Home and Oakland Cemetery.

Courtesy of John and Alvina Schaeffer

The first horse-drawn trolley starting on its initial trip up Columbus Avenue, 1883. The Great Western Band is playing. *Courtesy of Sandusky Library*

TRANSPORTATION

Wagon made by William Bing Carriage and Wagon Shop on Tiffin Avenue by Washington Street, circa 1885. *Courtesy of James A. Edwards*

Delivery wagon for the Mrs. Conrad Frank Bakery, circa 1895. *Courtesy of Sandusky Library*

H. Binns Gasoline and Coal Oil delivery wagon, 1883. The business was at Harrison and Monroe streets. *Courtesy of Sandusky Library*

George Schade in his electric auto, 1893. *Courtesy of Sandusky Library*

Foot of Columbus Avenue and Water Street, circa 1895. The excursion trains came here to take the passengers to the boats that took them to Cedar Point. *Courtesy of Katharine Schneider*

Lake Shore Electric Railway station in Huron, circa 1895. *Courtesy of Sandusky Library*

A Lake Shore & Michigan Southern steam locomotive taking on water at Sandusky, circa 1898. *Courtesy of Sandusky Library*

Businessmen on a launch owned by Koehler Bros. Meat Market to deliver meat to arriving lake freighters, circa 1900. *Courtesy of Janice M. Ross*

TRANSPORTATION

Avery Nickle Plate Depot, meeting spot of the Nickle Plate passenger train and Sandusky, Milan, & Norwalk interurban, circa 1900. The rail lines were feeders for each other. *Courtesy of Milan Historical Museum*

Big Four steam locomotive in Sandusky, circa 1900. *Courtesy of Sandusky Library*

Employees in front of the car barn of the Lake Shore Electric Railway Co. in Sandusky, 1902. *Courtesy of Sandusky Library*

Lake Shore Electric Railway employees on a handcar at Milan, circa 1905. *Courtesy of Sandusky Library*

Goosman Transfer Co., 1901. The business, located at 122 Wayne Street, began in the 1870s as Goosman Bros., operating omnibus lines to and from hotels and depots in Sandusky. An ad in the 1878 Sandusky Directory says "The best horses and Nobbiest Rigs furnished at the shortest notice." *Courtesy of Sandusky Library*

TRANSPORTATION

John, Lizzie, and Mike Bechberger in their Cadillac, the second car sold in Sandusky, 1906. *Courtesy of Katharine Schneider*

Henry Schmidt driving the grocery wagon making deliveries for the J. Bonn Grocery Co., circa 1909. *Courtesy of Janis Grathwol Burke*

The boat *Tourist* ran from Sandusky to the Lake Erie Islands, circa 1910. *Courtesy of Katharine Schneider*

Arrow shuttled passengers from Sandusky to the islands from 1895 to 1922. *Courtesy of Janice M. Ross*

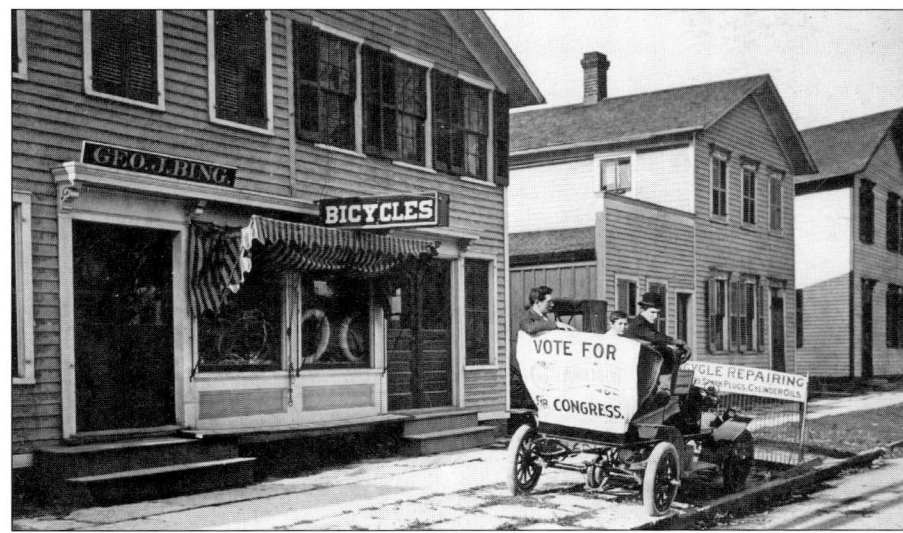
George J. Bing's bicycle and automobile supply store on Tiffin Avenue near Washington Street, circa 1910. The sign on the auto promotes the candidacy of Carl Anderson who served in the U.S. Congress from 1909 to 1912. *Courtesy of James A. Edwards*

Standard Oil wagon on Main Street, Huron, circa 1910. *Courtesy of Huron Historical Society*

Moving wine casks over Lake Erie, circa 1910. Wine was a major commodity produced in the Erie Isles. *Courtesy of Milan Historical Museum*

Delivery wagons in front of George J. Bing's bicycle and automobile supply store, circa 1910. *Courtesy of James A. Edwards*

George J. Bing built an airplane in his auto repair shop in 1912. He brought it over to the bay for its first flight but was unable to take off. *Courtesy of Sandusky Library*

Lake Shore & Michigan Southern Railroad depot in Sandusky, circa 1910. *Courtesy of Roger Dickman*

C.E. Nicholson Freight Transfer & Moving unloading a large lathe machine on Railroad Street, possibly for Sandusky Foundry & Machine, circa 1910. *Courtesy of Roger Dickman*

Adolf Kromer, Joseph Smith (born in 1827), and two unidentified men traveling in Perkins Township, circa 1915. It was Mr. Smith's first ride in an auto. *Courtesy of Audrey Harrison*

Leroy Weier at the wheel with the Milan Bridge in the background, circa 1915. *Courtesy of Sandusky Library*

One of Sandusky's locally built biplanes flying over the east end of Sandusky Bay, circa 1913. *Courtesy of Sandusky Library*

Biemiller's Garage at 240-242 Wayne Street, circa 1912. Capt. Otto Biemiller was the owner of one of Sandusky's earliest gas stations. *Courtesy of Roger Dickman*

A biplane at the Erie County Fairgrounds, circa 1915. Reinhart Ausmus was the pilot of the plane built in Sandusky by Tom Benoist who operated a flight school. *Courtesy of Sandusky Library*

Interior of West End Tire & Repair, 501 Tiffin Avenue, circa 1921. J.F. Bitter was the proprietor. *Courtesy of Roger Dickman*

Sandusky Gas and Electric Co. truck, circa 1925. *Courtesy of Sandusky Library*

Steamer *Put-in-Bay* that traveled between Put-in-Bay, Sandusky, and Detroit. The line began operating in 1911. *Courtesy of Sandusky Library*

TRANSPORTATION

At a Sandusky dock, circa 1915. The steamer *G.A. Boeckling* is on the left and the *Put-in-Bay* is docked on the right. *Courtesy of Sandusky Library*

Marvin Leech drove the taxi from the dock to the Hotel Victory at Put-in-Bay, 1916. *Courtesy of Don Leech*

A seaplane on Sandusky Bay, 1919. *Courtesy of Sandusky Library*

Frank Muenchow with one of the electric cars he drove at the Soldiers' and Sailors' Home, circa 1920. *Courtesy of Sheila Pfanne*

The Griswold-Wagg Motor Co. sold Ford automobiles in Sandusky on East Washington Row, circa 1920. *SCourtesy of Sandusky Library*

An early auto in downtown Sandusky, 1925. *Courtesy of Sandusky Library*

Lake Shore Electric Railway officials gathered to board car No. 182 for the inaugural run over the short Sandusky Connecting Railway as the Sandusky cut-off opened in 1926. The 2.5-mile line eliminated going through downtown Sandusky. *Courtesy of Sandusky Library*

Ice bridge on Sandusky Bay, 1935. *Courtesy of Sandusky Library*

Tip Top Auto Top Shop, McDonough and Washington streets, circa 1930. Morris Link, Sr., left, and Morris Link, Jr., were the owners. *Courtesy of Carol J. Matlock*

American Railway Express workers, 1927. *Courtesy of Sandusky Library*

Streetcar tracks being laid on Columbus Avenue, 1925. The original tracks were laid in 1883 for the horse-drawn trolleys. *Courtesy of Sandusky Library*

Car show in the Jackson Junior High School gym. 1927. The doorways of the building were designed to allow large items such as automobiles into the auditorium.
Courtesy of Nanette Guss

Steamer *Chippewa* at Sandusky dock at the foot of Columbus Avenue, circa 1930. The ferry ran to Put-in-Bay. *Courtesy of Huron Historical Society*

G.A. Boeckling at the dock at Cedar Point by the Cedars Hotel, 1940. One of the most popular steamers on the Great Lakes, the ship was named after George Boeckling, best known as the owner of the Cedar Point Amusement Park. The steamer was built in Ecorse, Michigan, in 1909. *Courtesy of Edward Sandrock*

Ships at the Sandusky coal docks, circa 1930. The ships, left to right: *C.H. McCullough, Jr.*, *Mariposa*, *Wm. A. Reiss*, *Merton E. Farr*, *Diamond Alkali*, and *A.T. Kinney*. *Courtesy of Sandusky Library*

TRANSPORTATION

Willys-Knight Overland at Harten Brooks Motor Co., Huron Avenue. *Courtesy of Deborah Neese-Voltz*

Filling station on East Monroe and Hancock streets, circa 1930. *Courtesy of Sandusky Library*

Island Air Lines used these Ford Trimotor airplanes, also known as the "Tin Goose," to shuttle passengers and cargo between the Lake Erie islands and the mainland beginning in the 1930s. *Courtesy of Lisa Benjamin*

Lake Erie & The Isles

"The chief products of Put-in-Bay are fish, flirtations, limestone and Perry's Victory," as quoted by an island observer in 1898.

Known for all these things, as well as the majestic but doomed Hotel Victory, South Bass Island began drawing visitors in the 1850s to sample the wines produced on the island and enjoy time away from the toils of home and work.

Kelleys Island is more sedate but has also served as a Mecca for those seeking a respite with natural attractions such as Inscription Rock — pictographic writings more than 500 years old — and one of the largest examples of glacial grooves left in the world. Early residents of the island engaged in the business of wine-making, quarrying, logging, fruit-growing and fishing.

Johnson's Island, across the bay from Sandusky, is now best known for its Confederate Soldiers' Cemetery but in the late 1800s, the Johnson's Island Pleasure Resort competed with Cedar Point for the summer recreation business.

View of Put-in-Bay harbor, circa 1920. The photographer was Ernst Niebergall. *Courtesy of Sandusky Library*

The second Huron light was built in 1857. *Courtesy of Huron Historical Society*

View of Put-in-Bay with Gibraltar Island in the background, circa 1880, from a stereographic card of the series by A.C. Platt. *Courtesy of Sandusky Library*

Officers' Headquarters at the Johnson's Island Civil War prison camp, circa 1890. *Courtesy of Sandusky Library*

Grand Pavilion and bandstand at Cedar Point, circa 1888, shortly after they opened. The first summer resort on Cedar Point began in 1870 and gained popularity in the 1880s. *Courtesy of Sandusky Library*

Glacial grooves on Kelleys Island, circa 1880. This portion of the grooves was quarried. *Courtesy of Sandusky Library*

The docks at Huron, circa 1890. *Courtesy of Sandusky Library*

Dock on Kelleys Island, circa 1885. *Courtesy of Sandusky Library*

Kelley's Island Wine Co., 1894. *Courtesy of Sandusky Library*

Frank Ritter, lighthouse keeper, and his family in front of the Sandusky Bay Front Range Light at Cedar Point, circa 1895. *Courtesy of Sandusky Library*

Quarries on Kelleys Island, circa 1900. *Courtesy of Sandusky Library*

Put-in-Bay Harbor, 1904. *Courtesy of Ed Spayd*

Crowd walking on the dock from the ferry toward Cedar Point, circa 1900. People traveled to Cedar Point by steamboats from cities on Lake Erie, including Sandusky, Toledo, Cleveland, and Detroit. During peak times, boats ran every half hour between Sandusky and Cedar Point. *Courtesy of Sandusky Library*

The Lake Shore Electric Railway stopped in front of the gates of Rye Beach Park, 1914. The park was approximately two miles west of Huron. *Courtesy of Sandusky Library and Huron Historical Society*

Hotel Victory at Put-in-Bay with the Victory Park Railway Terminal, circa 1905. Opened July 4, 1892, the hotel, with its 625 guest rooms and 1,000-seat dining room, was the largest resort hotel in America and featured the first coed swimming pool. It burned to the ground in 1919. *Courtesy of Ed Spayd*

The Pavilion, part of the resort on Johnson's Island, 1905. The Pavilion was built to replace the previous building which was destroyed by fire. It included a dancing pavilion and theater. It flourished for a season or two, but the owners of the competing resort acquired it and moved the buildings to Cedar Point. *Courtesy of Sandusky Library*

View of the Colonial amusement building on Put-in-Bay, built in 1905, that contained a bowling alley, restaurant, bar, and dance hall. *Courtesy of Sandusky Library*

Building the government pier at Huron, circa 1907. *Courtesy of Huron Historical Society*

Inscription Rock and a dock on Kelleys Island, circa 1909. *Courtesy of Sandusky Library*

Marblehead Lighthouse, winter of 1918. *Courtesy of Janis Grathwol Burke*

Vineyards on Kelleys Island, circa 1920. The photographer was Ernst Niebergall. *Courtesy of Sandusky Library*

Put-in-Bay East Point, likely showing the vineyards. Grapes were the main agricultural crop grown on the island. The photographer was Ernst Niebergall. *Courtesy of Sandusky Library*

ERIE COUNTY & THE ERIE ISLES

Sports & Leisure

Fishermen celebrate a great catch. A family picnics on Lake Erie. Gentlemen take in a ball game.

All the same leisure activities that occur today were just as popular 100 years ago. Some things, fortunately, never change.

Other elements, as depicted in the following pages, change drastically. The fishing crew and ball game spectators pictured, for example, are wearing neckties. The ladies are dressed properly to their chins and in most photos, wearing hats. Playing and bathing in the waters of Lake Erie called for just slightly less modesty.

Sports photos from the area include baseball, football, basketball and track teams, as well as more singular activities such as exhibition figure skating and ice boating.

Of particular note in this section are "The Harmonettes, Sandusky's first and only girl band" and what one might assume is the Kodak baseball team's mascot, but which actually belonged to the photographer and appears in other photos throughout the book. One might also wonder how they got him (or her) to wear a catcher's mask.

Enjoying the water at Cedar Point, circa 1900. *Courtesy of Sandusky Library*

SPORTS & LEISURE

Kromer family at Lake Erie, circa 1900. *Courtesy of Audrey Harrison*

A crowd watching the ball game at Kelleys Island, 1912. The man in the center with the big straw hat is Capt. Frank E. Hamilton. *Courtesy of Roger Dickman*

C.L. Engels Dry Goods Store picnic at Cedar Point, 1902. *Courtesy of Sandusky Library*

Fishermen gather at the dock to celebrate a good catch. The fish house was at the foot of Shelby Street. William Grathwol is standing on the right in the back row. *Courtesy of Janis Grathwol Burke*

Wieber family enjoying Crystal Rock beer, made by the Kuebeler-Stang Brewing Co., during a gathering at Cedar Point in the early 1900s. *Courtesy of Deborah Neese-Voltz*

SPORTS & LEISURE

Sandusky baseball team, 1908. Frank "Casey" Casserly is standing fourth from the left. *Courtesy of Julie Casserly and Nancy Roesch*

Employees of Cedar Point bath house, 1910. Ralph Ross is seventh from the left in the second row, Elsie Ross is on the left in the top row, and Harry Ward is seventh from the left in the top row. The four men in the top row were lifeguards. *Courtesy of Janice M. Ross*

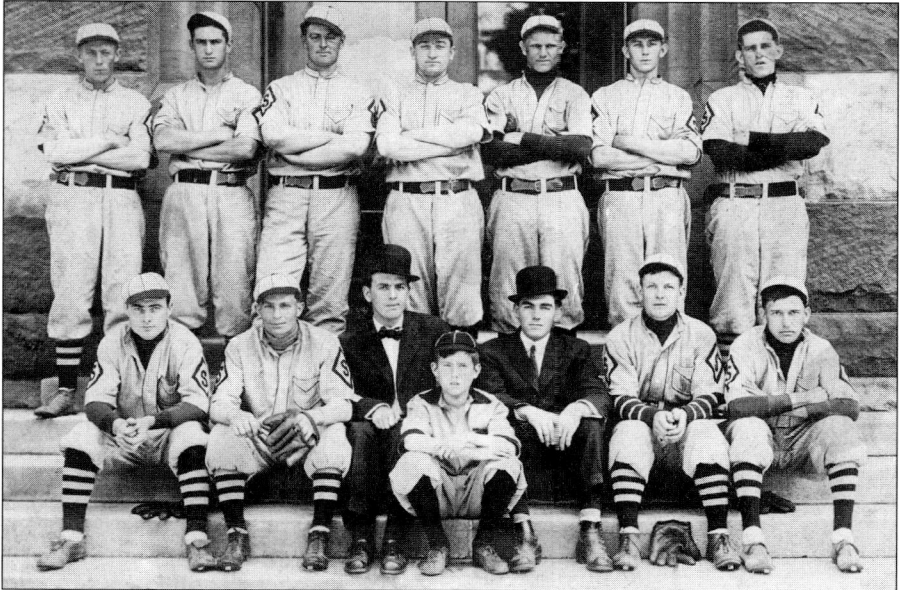

Shamrock baseball team, 1912 champions, seated on the Sandusky High School steps. Frank "Casey" Casserly, manager, is seated fourth from the left in the suit and top hat. *Courtesy of Julie Casserly and Nancy Roesch*

Horse racing on Central Avenue in Sandusky, circa 1910. *Courtesy of Sandusky Library*

Sandusky Acrobatic Group, 1916. Glenn Hommel is on the left and his father, William Hommel, manager of the Hommel Wine Company, is on the far right. Also included are Frank Pietschman, Carl Moos, and "Niks" Bier. *Courtesy of Mary Alice Appell*

Huron Parks baseball team, 1912. Frank Pietschman is on the right in the bottom row behind the man leaning on his elbow. *Courtesy of Mary Alice Appell*

Sailboat *Psamiad*, in the front, racing on Sandusky Bay, 1918. *Courtesy of Katharine Schneider*

SPORTS & LEISURE

Wiedenhafers' sports outing at Big Island, Sunday, May 16, 1915. The man in the middle with the mustache and high hat is Alfred Schnurr, Sr., builder and contractor. *Courtesy of Janet M. Schnurr Kerber*

Sandusky Maroons, a semi-professional football team, circa 1915. Wesley Till is on the left in the back row. *Courtesy of Bettyann Guss*

Bathing at Cedar Point Beach, circa 1920. Norman Ohlemacher is standing on the far right. Elsie Roberts Ohlemacher is fourth from the left in the front row. *Courtesy of Donald Ohlemacher*

Holzaepfel Kodaks baseball team, circa 1915. *Courtesy of Ed Boose*

Holzaepfel Kodaks baseball team, circa 1915. *Courtesy of Ed Boose*

Sandusky Business College basketball players, 1917. *Courtesy of Sandusky Library*

1922 Sandusky High School football team. On the left is coach Gosnell Layman. The players include: Bradford Granfield, Carl Bordus, Abe Cohn, Gilbert Barth, Stanley Walton, Henry Krebs, Hurland Dean, Vincent Lorenzen, Charles Edmund, Edwin Sprau, Clarence Voight, James Nicholson, Bryce White, Gary Salmon, Curtis Krebs, George Wagner, and Roland Reutler. *Courtesy of Roger Dickman*

SPORTS & LEISURE

Mike Bechberger's Snow Flake class ice boat was 30 feet long and the mast was 28 feet high, circa 1920. *Courtesy of Katharine Schneider*

Getting ready for a wolf hunt at Castalia, March 5, 1924. Sheriff Taylor was in charge of the hunt. *Courtesy of Audrey Harrison*

Sandusky High School track team, circa 1920. Included are Joe Payne, Leon Weichel, Glen Schropp, Joe Dempsey, and coach Sly. *Courtesy of Sandusky Library*

Playing in Lake Erie, circa 1930. Flo Leedom, with glasses, is second from the left. Her sister, Myrtle Patterson, is in the inner tube. *Courtesy of Becky Coleman*

St. Mary's seventh-grade basketball team, 1927. Front row, left to right: N. Windau, F. Roth, I. Obergefell, captain F. Lill, F. Hennrick, P. Gundlach, and D. Sartor. Back row: L. Brengartner, K. Brengartner, R. Schopp, L. Groff, H. Noe, E. Jump, and J. Olemacher. *Courtesy of Stephen J. Sartor*

Sandusky Business College basketball team, 1920-21. Front row, left to right: ___ Gysan, unknown, Willard Grathwol, Russel Dorr, and unknown. Back row: Harry Miller, Amos Strong, Mr. Wollenslagel, unknown, and Harry Siehl. *Courtesy of Janis Grathwol Burke*

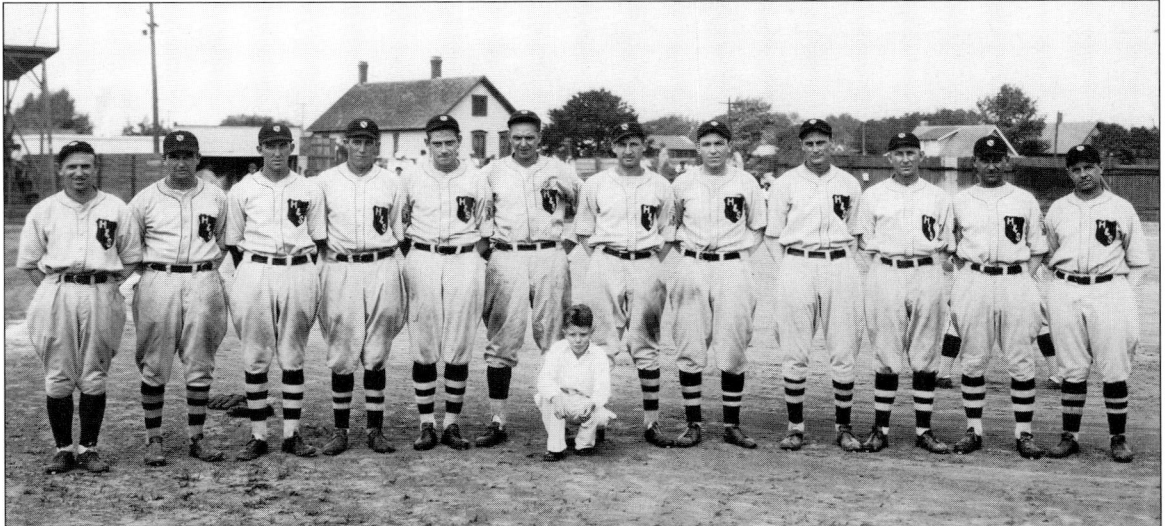

H & S Baking team played baseball at the Farrell-Cheek Ball Park on Perkins Avenue, circa 1929. They wore woolen uniforms donated by the Cleveland Indians. From left to right: Carl Bloker, Dutz Thompson, Willard Grathwol, Al Tigges, Red Sharp, Alva Halt, Reggie Kotz, Rol Gegner, Clyde Sharp, George Dahm, Walt Knupke, and Bucky Schwerer. *Courtesy of Janis Grathwol Burke*

SPORTS & LEISURE

Sandusky High School football team, 1920. *Courtesy of Sandusky Library*

Huron High School varsity basketball team, 1930. Back row, left to right: coach R.L. McCormick, Art Gall, Mark Somershield, Carl Ebert, Rockie Larizza, and T.W. Hartley. Front: Alder Nagy, Charles Zimmerman, Bill Frye, Mack Hayes, and Paul Rhodes. *Courtesy of Aileen Hartley*

Sandusky High School championship team, 1931. Front row, left to right: Johnice Turner, Lois Skillman, Elizabeth Wild, Inez Sturzinger, and Leona Jevas. Back row: coach Miss Lois Everett, Wilda Eger, Dorothy Rohde, and Winifred Close. *Courtesy of Ann Hoehne*

Fishing shanties on frozen Lake Erie from Kafralu Island toward Battery Park, 1937. *Courtesy of Bob Weichel*

Yost baseball team, circa 1935. Al Yost, owner of Bogart Garage at Milan and Bogart roads, is kneeling in front with his twins, Alice and Rosie. Players from left to right: Harold Sherwood, Lee Lundy, unknown, Andy Groesch, Johnny Rhinemiller, Joe Yost, Sr., unknown, Ed Simons, Lawrence Tight, Rol Simons, and Art David. *Courtesy of Joseph F. Yost III*

View of an early regatta taken from a launch toward Cedar Point, circa 1939. *Courtesy of Bob Weichel*

Wesley L. Till performing exhibition figure skating at the ice carnival at Battery Park, circa 1939. *Courtesy of Mary Ellen Till Fletcher*

The Harmonettes, billed as Sandusky's first and only girl band. Left to right: Florence (Brengartner) Roth, Thelma (Brengartner) Weise, Dorothy Hartsook, LaVesta (Muenchow) Amolsch, Hildegard (Erney) Stockdale, and Marcella (Erney) Pierce. *Courtesy of Sheila Pfanner*

EVENTS

Presidential campaigns, parades, church dedications, visits from luminaries — all these things bring a community together. The following pages reflect the spirit of celebration, devotion, pride and, perhaps — in the case of the elephant parade, at least — the curiosity of the people who populated early Erie County.

The community is called to come together too, when disaster strikes. This section provides a glimpse at some of those occasions:

A 1909 fire in Huron, which destroyed the Leonhiser building, the Odd Fellows Temple and the Garulich Bakery.

The Mahala Block fire, also in 1909, which spread so fast in downtown Sandusky that most occupants escaped with only the clothes they were wearing.

The tornado of 1924, which struck Sandusky and Lorain without warning on a hot June afternoon, causing widespread devastation and killing eight in Sandusky, 72 in Lorain.

But communities always come together again, to regroup and rebuild, creating new cause for celebration.

And always, memories and photos remain.

Knights of St. John parade on Columbus Avenue, 1910. *Courtesy of Sandusky Library*

Circus elephants parading at Camp Street and Tiffin Avenue, circa 1890. *Courtesy of Deborah Neese-Voltz*

The Bishop of Ohio, the Rt. Rev. William A. Leonard, laid the cornerstone of Calvary Episcopal Church, First and Meigs streets, on September 17, 1899. *Courtesy of James Arthur*

U.S. President Taft speaking at the Soldiers' and Sailors' Home in Sandusky, 1908. *Courtesy of Sandusky Library*

Ice storm on Meigs Street, 1909. *Courtesy of Amelia Davlin*

Laying the cornerstone of Zion's new church building at Columbus Avenue and West Jefferson Street, August 21, 1898. Pastor August Dornbirer is holding an open Bible behind the man handling the cornerstone. *Courtesy of Laura Stellhorn*

Mahala Block fire, November 18, 1909. The fire caused nearly $250,000 in damages, destroying many businesses and apartments. William T. West built the Mahala Block in 1892 on East Washington Row. *Courtesy of Sandusky Library*

EVENTS

A fire in Huron, June 12, 1909. The photo was taken shortly after the Sandusky Fire Department arrived at the scene at 7:30 a.m. and shows the Leonhiser building. Other buildings destroyed included the Odd Fellows Temple and the Graulich Bakery where the fire started. *Courtesy of Roger Dickman*

Teddy Roosevelt, running for president, made a whistle-stop in Sandusky, May 15, 1912. Sandusky Mayor George T. Lehrer is on the far left. *Courtesy of Sandusky Library*

A large crowd gathered as Glenn Curtiss flew from Euclid Beach in Cleveland to Cedar Point over Lake Erie, setting the record for the longest flight over water on August 31, 1910. *Courtesy of Sandusky Library*

Downtown Sandusky decorated for the Perry's Victory Centennial, September 1913. The event celebrated Commodore Perry's victory over the British during the War of 1812 in a battle fought near Put-in-Bay. *Courtesy of Sandusky Library*

EVENTS

"Niagara," Commodore Perry's flagship during the war of 1812, was restored and present in Sandusky in 1913 for the 100th anniversary celebration of Perry's victory over the British Fleet in the War of 1812. The Battle of Lake Erie was fought in the waters around Put-in-Bay near Sandusky. *Courtesy of Gary Kelley*

Flower mounds in Washington Park for the Perry Centennial, 1913. *Courtesy of Sandusky Library*

Tornado damage on Water Street from the B&O Railroad to the end, 1924. The tornado occurred on the afternoon of June 28, destroying a portion of downtown

Charles Evans Hughes in Sandusky during his campaign for president, September 26, 1916. He spoke outside the American Crayon Co. factory. *Courtesy of Sandusky Library*

The Lake Shore Tire Co. float for a Fourth of July parade, 1919. *Courtesy of Sandusky Library*

and killing eight people. The tornado traveled along the lakeshore, all the way to Lorain where 72 people were killed. *Courtesy of Arnold and Jean Mischler*

Thomas Edison, Henry Ford, and Harvey Firestone at the Milan town square, 1923. They had been in Marion for the funeral of U.S. President Warren G. Harding. This was Edison's last visit to his hometown. *Courtesy of Milan Historical Museum*

Tornado forces overturned this automobile resting across a boat slip along Sandusky Bay, June 28, 1924. *Courtesy of Nanette Guss*

Tornado destruction along Sandusky Bay, June 28, 1924. *Courtesy of Nanette Guss*

Tornado damage, 1924. *Courtesy of Sandusky Library*

PUBLIC SERVICE

That Sandusky is Erie County's public seat is attributed more to accident than design. In 1838, the selection commission toured Huron and Sandusky, both contenders for the designation. During their Huron visit, a storm came up and a great area of lowland was rendered impassable, stranding the commission for several hours.

Conversely, their trip to Sandusky found one of the largest lake vessels of the day riding safely in the waters of Sandusky Bay, having sought refuge during the storm. The commission voted unanimously in favor of Sandusky. The Erie County Court House was completed in 1874.

In 1886, the Ohio legislature authorized the creation of the Ohio Soldiers' and Sailors' Home in Perkins Township to provide for Ohio's indigent, honorably discharged veterans from the Civil War. More than 50,000 veterans from various U.S. conflicts have resided at the home, which is now known as the Ohio Veterans Home.

The following pages feature photos of both facilities, as well as early fire and police departments and other public services.

Sandusky Fire Department on Central Avenue in front of St. Mary's Church, circa 1910. The first professional fire department in Sandusky was organized in 1883. *Courtesy of Sandusky Library*

Soldiers' and Sailors' Home, circa 1890. The facility opened in 1888 admitting 17 veterans. On the right is the administration building. *Courtesy of Sandusky Library*

Huron Volunteer Fire Department, circa 1895. Chief was Henry Schafer, their driver was George Knott. *Courtesy of Huron Historical Society*

Erie County Courthouse, circa 1895. Built in 1874 of limestone and sandstone, the building was remodeled in the 1930s. *Courtesy of Sandusky Library*

Decorated for the funeral of Adam E. Hartung, captain of the No. 4 Hose Wagon, March 1908. Capt. Hartung died from injuries suffered falling from a horse wagon on the way to a fire on November 11, 1907. *Courtesy of Sandusky Library*

Providence Hospital opened in 1902, founded by the Sisters of Charity in the former home of C.C. Keech on Hayes Avenue. *Courtesy of John and Alvina Schaeffer*

U.S. President William Howard Taft riding in a car with his friend, Edward Marsh, at the Soldiers' and Sailors' Home, September 8, 1908. *Courtesy of Sandusky Library*

A Sandusky fire engine, June 12, 1909, at a fire in Huron. The engine was stationed at the back of the mill south of the Lake Shore Electric Railway Company bridge. From there 1,100 feet of hose was laid to the fire. *Courtesy of Roger Dickman*

Unveiling of the monument at the Confederate cemetery on Johnson's Island, 1910. *Courtesy of Sandusky Library*

PUBLIC SERVICE

Post office workers, 1912. Included are: Harry Schmminger, Jim McCann, Tim Ryan, John Schaub, Harry Gosser, Postmaster Charles Schippel, Ed Ernst, Dan Schwab, Louis Holzauer, Bill Twiggs, and Roman Ott. *Courtesy of Sandusky Library*

Women of Zion Lutheran Church, working in the church basement, did Red Cross sewing during World War I. *Courtesy of Laura Stellhorn*

Gathering for a farewell party for J.J. Crecelius, a former Erie County Commissioner, at his home on Strecker Road in Oxford Township, September 17, 1917.

Sandusky postal employees at Jim Gillet's retirement party, circa 1910. Included are: Lewis Holzhauer, Norm Bitter, Charles Wilhelm, Jim Davis, Weldon Hein, R. Ott, William Gilbert, John Schaub, Williams Twiggs, Jim Gillet, Mrs. Gillet, Henry Schimminger, Jim McCann, Cliff Garner, Dan Schwab, Arthur Rudolph, and Ed Ernst. *Courtesy of Bill Arthur*

Erie County Clerk of Courts, Ferd J. Bing, circa 1925. *Courtesy of Amelia Davlin*

Courtesy of John and Alvina Schaeffer

U.S. Customs agent Kerwick Ryan destroying bootleg liquor, 1929. *Courtesy of Huron Historical Society*

Sandusky Police Department, July 1924. Left to right: William Schmidt, George Leitz, Edward Smith, R.G. Bravard, Al Tremper, Henry Scherer, Otto Rudolph, Capt. John Hobert, Al Bitzer, Capt. Henry Ringholtz, Capt. Leo Schiefley, Capt. Jay C. Perry, William Strauss, John Molz, Gus David, Conrad Hobert, and Capt. Peter Herb. *Courtesy of Sandusky Library*

EDUCATION

Erie County is a prominent figure in the history pages of education. Sandusky was one of the first cities in Ohio to have a high school and under the guidance of progressive educator M.F. Cowdery, a graded education system was inaugurated there in 1848. Students of all ages assembled and were assigned to one of four grades: primary, secondary, grammar or high school, setting a precedent for the state of Ohio. One year later, graded school became mandatory by state law.

High school subjects at the time included reading, writing, arithmetic, grammar, geography, Latin, French, philosophy, chemistry and physiology. Cleanliness and morality were stressed and the reading of the King James Bible was practiced at the beginning of school every morning.

Due to the number of local settlers with German heritage, German was, at one time, taught as an optional subject in Sandusky elementary schools, and those not taking it were subject to an extra half-hour of arithmetic each day, making German a very popular language.

Venice School, circa 1895. *Courtesy of Sandusky Library*

EDUCATION

Sandusky High School graduating class, circa 1865. *Courtesy of Sandusky Library*

Sandusky High School, circa 1890. The school was built in 1869. *Courtesy of Sandusky Library*

Students on the steps of Campbell School, circa 1890. *Courtesy of Sandusky Library*

Sandusky High School class of 1898. *Courtesy of Sandusky Library*

Put-in-Bay School, 1909. *Courtesy of Don Leech*

Sandusky High School graduating class of 1907: Glenn Cullen, Fred Groch, Elsa Pusch, Kenneth Kugel, Gene Ruth, Clara Rall, Fleeta Osgood, Lulu Owen, Pearl Frederick, Harry Dunn, Margaret Scott, Lenore Schoepfle, Bart Reinheimer, Beth Schumacher, Florence Cheney, Margarite Molitor, Josephine Muencher, Gussie Bookmeyer, Frank Wangler, Henrietta Nolan, Rosnette Manner, Edna Becker, and Viva Williams. *Courtesy of Sandusky Library*

Sandusky High School orchestra of 1904. Front, left to right: Verna Murphy and Edna Becker. Second row: George Lehrer, Bessie Lawrence, Theresa Winkler, and Cornelius Schnaitter. Back: Maude Clauss, Ralph Scherz, and Margaret Andrews. *Courtesy of Sandusky Library*

EDUCATION

Huron High School was built in 1886. The gym was housed on the third floor.
Courtesy of Huron Historical Society

Sandusky High School commencement, class of 1912. Helen Schaeffer is on the left in the front row. *Courtesy of John and Alvina Schaeffer*

Third grade, Madison School, 1919. Virginia Schmidt is fourth from the right in the front row. She became Virginia Schmidt Grathwol and served as Erie County Treasurer for 34 years. *Courtesy of Janis Grathwol Burke*

Campbell School seventh graders, 1919. Front row, left to right: Howard Brown, Ross Brown, Linn Pelton, Allen Stuffield, Wilbert Strack, Ellwood Appel, Douglas _____, Dallas Wolf, Max Burrow, Al Holzhouzer, and Charles Higgins. Second row: Albert Burrow, Eugene Zorn, Florence Peterson, Dorothy McKeen, Ruth Baumgarter, Marie _____, Illa Ward, Selma Wensher, LaNor Vessey, William Yoos, Robert Ruff, Frederick Alstedder, John Stubid, Margaret Curr, _____ Peters, Susan Mees, _____ Homberger, Augusta Burrow, and Roland Hess. Third row: Marguerite Canfield, Mildred Hessler, Dorothy Marthers, Ruth Herman, Elizabeth Strobel, Virginia James, Thelma Klein, Charolotte Huff, LaVesta Muenchow, and Betty Osborne. *Courtesy of Sheila Pfanner.*

Eighth-grade class at Milan School, 1921. Front row, left to right: Florence Sands, Kathryn Weilnau, Olive Wallrabenstein, Florence Mellein, Laura Morrow, and Gladys Schafer. Sitting: Clarence Grose, Manford Hosford, and teacher Miss Roberts. Middle row: Marjorie Milliman, John Drake, Paul Gano, James McLane, Paul Hauple, Lyle Schafer, and John Fox. Included in the back row: Calvin Wallrabenstein, Kenneth Strong, Donald Mason, Fred Meyers, Leslie _____, and Delbert Thayer. *Courtesy of John and Alvina Schaeffer.*

Venice School, a two-story, two-room schoolhouse on Venice Road next to the New York Central Railroad that bordered Sandusky Bay, circa 1920. The schoolhouse served students in grades one through eight. Teacher Anna Gysan, far left in the back row, taught students in grades one through three. Principal D.W. Carlisle, far right in the back row, taught students in grades four through eight. Louis Zeller is the tallest boy to the left of Mr. Carlisle. The schoolhouse remained in use until 1922 when a new school was built on Bardshar Road. *Courtesy of Evelyn Zeller.*

Sandusky High School class of 1918. Zelma Collins is fourth from the right in the second row. *Courtesy of Edward Sandrock*

Graduation celebration by the Sandusky High School class of 1920. Graduates include: Cecil Kline, Earl Seitz, Ruth Baumeister, Frank Kastor, Willard Jahraus, Owen Nicholson, Marie Pfanner, Mildred Burge, Elizabeth Hinde, Antoinette Link, Kathryn Windisch, Helen Grob, Henrietta Knauer, Rose Jewett, Marie Loeffler, Lottie Schroder, Christine Schade, Dorothy Wiegel, Juanita Wiles, Antoinette Gundlach, Sabina Murray, Eleanor Stutz, Dorothy Curtis, Miss Denham, Al Simon, Mary Appell, Lynn Rosino, Jim Brown, Margaret Schumacher, Wilber Schwer, Carl Deist, Helen Rheinegger, Ruth Beach, Raymond Heinzerling, Vera Bornhauser, Dorthy Sturm, Elsie Sehlmeyer, Eloise Ross, Esther Brown, Kathryn Muray, Gladys Bickley, Ruth Schaeffer, Edna Scheid, Caroline Taylor, Agnes McClaren, Lucille Proy, Marjorie McKean, Loise Dusold, Carl Miller, and Sidney Knehr. *Courtesy of Sandusky Library*

EDUCATION

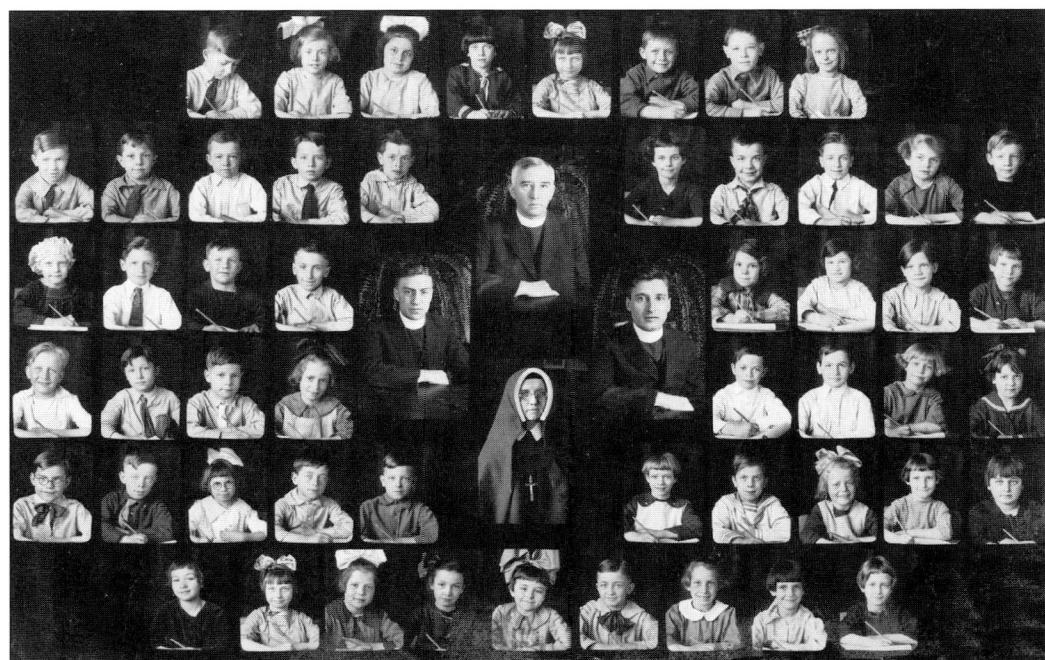

St. Mary's third-grade class, 1923. Top row, left to right: R. Loeffler, M. Baum, H. Curtis, R. Cudaro, C. Munder, N. Windau, C. Schemmer, and unknown. Second row: M. Oberle, J. Olemacher, L. Lempke, C. Hindeland, I. Obergefell, E. Gerhardstein, L. Hohler, J. Geismarr, M. Nesselhauf, and M. Malone. Third row: V. Missig, F. Lill, J. Hemrick, F. Kieffer, M. Schaefer, unknown, R. Holzmiller, and unknown. Fourth row: E. Oswald, S. Spalla, D. Sartor, Z. Ringholz, C. Kaman, N. Ferback, A. Meyer, and M. Scheid. Fifth row: D. Kantz, E. Jump, M. Buck, N. Schwanger, K. Brengartner, M. Englehorn, E. Sheck, F. Ringholz, K. Gaydish, and E. Simwald. Sixth row: R. Lemke, unknown, M. Olemacher, unknown, D. Weisler, F. Perla, unknown, R. Gadish, and B. Rorh. Center: Fr. Zieroff, unknown, unknown, and Sr. Mary Rosemarie. *Courtesy of Stephen J. Sartor*

Portraits of the 1919 graduating class, Sandusky High School. *Courtesy of Marlene Roberts*

A gathering of Sandusky school children at the entrance to Sandusky High School, circa 1925. *Courtesy of Karen and Robert Deitz*

Sandusky High School Band in front of the school, 1923. This was the school's first band. *Courtesy of Sheila Pfanner*

St. Mary's eighth-grade class, 1929. *Courtesy of Stephen J. Sartor*

Third-grade class band with their teacher, Ethel Leber. John Schaeffer is in the middle row, fourth from the left; Alvina Crecelius is in the back row fourth from the right. *Courtesy of John and Alvina Schaeffer*

Sycamore School, circa 1935. *Courtesy of James Arthur*

EDUCATION

Sandusky High School Band, circa 1930. *Courtesy of Sandusky Library*

Senior class, Mr. Fleming's homeroom, Sandusky High School, 1940. *Courtesy of Dr. John K. Schaefer*

Kindergarten class at Osborne School with their teacher, Mrs. Isaac, 1940. *Courtesy of Anna Fantozzi*

Sandusky High School Band, April 1936. *Courtesy of Bill Werner*

SOCIETY

According to the old adage, a picture is worth a thousand words, but it seems words are sometimes necessary to complete the illustration.

In this section, for example, the photo of the Amolsch home interior would be incomplete without details of how one "smuggled" doll became a family heirloom.

In the following pages, barns are built, neighborhood playmates are are reunited and war veterans are recognized. Prams, picnics and ponies are pictured and the Pietschman girls get their weekly beach time. The Shannon brothers pose with their musical instruments, the Caramagnos are wed, goat-drawn carts are popular, as is watermelon in the summertime.

These pictures, and their accompanying text, tell stories of the Erie County we remember in years past.

Crecelius home on Bryan Road, Milan Township, 1910. Herman and Mary Ohlemacher Crecelius stand with their children: Albert on the pony, Paul in the buggy, and Arvata by the bear. The other woman is Edith Hart. *Courtesy of John and Alvina Schaeffer*

Minnie Kromer and friends sampling watermelon on the Kromer farm on Ohio 4 in Perkins Township, circa 1900. *Courtesy of Audrey Harrison*

Peter Yepsen family, 1901, lived on Perkins Avenue in Sandusky. *Courtesy of Paul M. Ward*

Cora and Minnie Kromer are part of this group at Cedar Point, circa 1905. *Courtesy of Audrey Harrison*

Emma Grathwol in her wicker pram, 1901. She was born November 19, 1899, to William and Lina Stookey Grathwol. *Courtesy of Janis Grathwol Burke*

Children of John and Mary Schultz Schaeffer, circa 1908. *Courtesy of John and Alvina Schaeffer*

Lois Ford, age 12, in 1900. Lois lived in Groton Township. *Courtesy of Edward Sandrock*

Interior of the Frank and Annette Muenchow home, 223 Finch Street, Sandusky, 1912. The statue doll on the mantle was grabbed by their daughter and hidden under her blanket while riding in a wagon through a store. Her mother discovered she had taken it when they got home. She took it back to the store but the owner said they could keep it. The doll became a family keepsake for years to come. *Courtesy of Sheila Pfanner*

SOCIETY

John A. Koehler home at 323 Perry Street was built in 1900. Koehler's oldest daughter is standing on the walk. *Courtesy of Janice M. Ross*

Doller cottage, Put-in-Bay, 1900. *Courtesy of Don Leech*

The Michel home, owner of Michel Bros. Cooperage, on the southeast corner of East Market and Franklin streets, 1890. *Courtesy of Janice M. Ross*

Building a barn for Jacob Crecelius, Strecker Road, Oxford Township, 1910. *Courtesy of John and Alvina Schaeffer*

Picnic on the Kromer farm, Ohio 4, Perkins Township, circa 1915. *Courtesy of Audrey Harrison*

LaVesta Muenchow Amolsch and Ed Wilkins on a trip to Lakeside, May 24, 1924. *Courtesy of Sheila Pfanner*

Otto and Nettie Kerber with their children, Cecelia and Henry, 1914. Mr. Kerber owned Kerber Marine Grocery. *Courtesy of Nancy Roesch*

On the way to Sunday School at Calvary Episcopal Church are siblings Nellie and Juanita Gilbert in the front with Helen and Wilbur in the back, 1917. The horse is Snookie. The Gilberts lived at 1317 Prospect Street. *Courtesy of James Arthur*

On the beach at Cedar Point, circa 1920. Front row, left to right: Victor Weis, Ferd W. Bing, and Carl Zimmerman. Middle row: Marion Ueberle and Virginia Bing. Back row: Ferd J. Bing and Amelia Bing. *Courtesy of Amelia Davlin*

Birthday party for Mildred and Ruth Pietschman, second from the right in the bottom row and second from the right in the third row, at the Sandusky Children's Home, 1922. *Courtesy of Mary Alice Appell*

Walter "Bud" and Ida Marie with their mother, Anna Marie Luipold, in O'Donald's Woods, sailing a boat made by their father, Martin, summer 1929. Martin owned a barber shop on Hayes Avenue for fifty years. Walter was killed in Normandy during World War II. *Courtesy of Robert S. Guss, Sr.*

Juanita and Eileen Toft in their yard at 1413 W. Taylor Street, 1927. *Courtesy of Gary R. Mussell*

Children of William P. and Hilda Harris, 1927. Left to right: Bill, Donald, Jack, and Betty. *Courtesy of Robert and Karen Deitz*

Shannon brothers, sons of Lois Ford, at Cedar Point Ohio Band Camp, 1933. *Courtesy of Edward Sandrock*

Doris Betty Patterson and Robert L. Patterson on the Patterson farm east of Huron off U.S. 6, circa 1930. *Courtesy of Becky Coleman*

Valentine A. Fries, III, Milan High School, 1939. He was one of three Erie County men killed in the Battle of the Bulge, winter of 1944. *Courtesy of John and Alvina Schaeffer*

Carr Street playmates, circa 1935, left to right: Pete Lococo, Don Gibeaut, Chuck Gibeaut, Jean Thomas, and Jim Roberts. *Courtesy of Marlene Roberts*

Home of Robert L. and Myrtle Patterson east of Huron on U.S. 6, circa 1935. *Courtesy of Becky Coleman*

Bremer, Zuelzke, and Guckert families on a Cedar Point outing, circa 1936. They are sitting along the boardwalk with the "Joy Plane" in the background and the bath house to the right. *Courtesy of Marlene Roberts*

Summer home of Jay Cooke on Gibraltar Island, circa 1930. Jay Cooke was born in Sandusky in 1821 and became a successful financier during his career, being referred to as the financier of the Civil War. He purchased Gibraltar Island in 1864 and built a home there as a retreat for his family. *Courtesy of Sandusky Library*

Frank and Christine Pietschman's girls on Cedar Point, 1932. From left to right: Martha, Mary Alice, Lois, Grace, Ruth, Mildred, and mother, Christine. The Pietschmans owned a shoe store on Tiffin Avenue but managed to visit Cedar Point at least once a week to enjoy the beach, have a picnic, and ride on the rides. *Courtesy of Mary Alice Appell*

Wedding of Yolanda and Sam Caramagno, circa 1935. The ring bearer is Sam Glorioso. The flower girl on the left is Josephine Glorioso. *Courtesy of Gary Kelley*

COMMUNITY

The following pages are filled with images that reflect a wide variety of special interest groups, clubs and organizations. Residents of Erie County and the Erie Isles have, throughout history, been drawn to reach out to the larger community, with like-minded individuals, to beautify and better the area.

The Maccabee Society, the Marquette Club, bible classes, choirs and church guilds are some of the groups represented in this section. The first Boy Scout troop in Sandusky is pictured, as are the top 10 finishers in the Ohio Beauty Pageant at Cedar Point in 1927. Miss Beryl Starr of Sandusky appears in this photo displayed in this section.

Also included are images of the buildings, boulevards and parks where the community has, and continues to, come together.

Members of Zion Lutheran Church's Vestry, or Church Council, 1927. Front row, left to right: Ed Maeder, Frank Schlolttag, Rev. Theodore J.C. Stellhorn, August O. Gast, August Troike, and Frank Luce. Back row: Harry Fowles, Ed Bunge, Martin Luberger, Ralph Rodisel, Al Arheit, William Harpst, Frank Papenfuss, and Charles W. Schmidt.
Courtesy of Laura Stellhorn

COMMUNITY

Maccabee Society, circa 1900, Bloomingville. *Courtesy of Audrey Harrison*

Zion Lutheran Church members singing at a patriotic community event at the Carnegie Library, circa 1900. The director was George Lehrer. *Courtesy of Laura Stellhorn*

Thomas Edison homeplace before the wrap-around porch was added in 1898. *Courtesy of Milan Historical Museum*

First Boy Scout troop in Sandusky camping in a shanty called "the crow's nest" on Cedar Point near Biemiller Cove, circa 1910. Scouts, from the top of the ladder: Wesley Till, Clarence Stockdale, Harold Till, Harold Stockdale, Harold Gerold, and Eugene Close. Their scout master was Dr. Charles Stroud, a local dentist who had served as captain of Company B during the Spanish-American War. *Courtesy of Bettyann Guss*

First concert given by St. Mary's choir, February 9, 1911. Front row, left to right: I. Fox, J. Singler, P. Singler, G. Erne, unknown, H. Fox, M. Zeller, conductor N. Fox, L. Neis, H. Klueg, A. Grathwol, and L. Klueg. Second row: I. Goodwin, M. Scifman, M. Braun, J. Olrini, O. Gundlach, M. Seiler, L. Seymour, R. Grathwol, M. Bauman, E. Scales, M. Williams, B. Belz, A. Herb, and C. Fox. Third row: unknown, L. Scheck, unknown, unknown, M. Kessler, V. Frick, C. Enilse, A. Frick. L. Gaehert, M. Kraus, L. Herzog, M. Bighn, L. Houk, M. Missig, S. Missig, and O. Missig. Back row: J. Missig, J. Schein, F. Frey, unknown, W. Schaefer, G. Young, N. Erne, unknown, unknown, A. Biehl, L. Iscman, C. Sartor, N. Houk, J. Mayer, W. Busam, E. Busam, and W. Trost. *Courtesy of Stephen J. Sartor*

Adult bible class at St. Stephen's Evangelical German Church, Pastor H.E. Phieffer, 1920. Front row, left to right: Mrs. Taber, Mrs. Wendschuh, unknown, Ida Schmid, unknown, Mrs. Ohle, unknown, Oscar Wendschuh, Mrs. Siehl, Jacob Beier, Mrs. Wendschuh, Elsie Braun, Mrs. Zimmerman, Lucille Fettel, Christ Mayer, Arnold Ehrsam, Maurice Bahnsen, Pastor Pheiffer, unknown, Rol Bauman, John Braun, Jake Stoffal, Edwin Braun, John Kunze, and Henry Gassan. Second row: Molly Hankhamer, unknown, unknown, Mrs. Firby, Mrs. Barz, Ann Stoffal, and Frieda Soaff. Back row: Augusta Bechtel, Helen Schweitzer, Mrs. Mischler, Mrs. Stoffal, Florence Braun, Mrs. Mayer, Mrs. Arheit, Mrs. Rudolph, Mrs. Ohle, and Mrs. Fettal. *Courtesy of Janis Grathwol Burke*

Altar boys at St. Mary's Church Sanctuary, 1925. *Courtesy of Stephen J. Sartor*

Second communion and confirmation at St. Mary's Church, 1922. Lola Lange is fifth from the left in the first row. *Courtesy of Marilyn J. Ward*

St. Stephen's Evangelical German Church confirmation class, 1921. Pastor Harry Pheiffer with confirmands: Catherine Maus, Jennie Troike, Ione Bechtel, Janet Sharp, Esther Walker, Selma Wendschuh, Mildred Sommers, Harold Redman, Theo "Chas" Gettle, Elmer Ohly, Arnold Stein, Alvin Bechtel, Pastor Pheiffer, Stuart Ohly, and Merley Sharp. One of the boys is unknown. *Courtesy of Janis Grathwol Burke*

Girls Chorus of Zion Lutheran Church, circa 1927. Front row, left to right: Mildred Dunkle, Irene Melville, Emily Piper, Florence Hankamer, director Harriet Reinheimer, Matilda Boison, Ruth Steinert, and Ida Patch. Middle row: Jeannette Otto, Frieda Knupke, Eloise Marquardt, Caroline Thiede, Elsie Heinsen, unknown, Dorothy Winkle, Bertha Piper, Marie Papke, and Marion Rose. Back row: Edith Bartels, Thelma Staffler, Loretta Zech, Hannah Kiether, Arlene Ziemke, Emeline Zemke, Mildred Kauer, and Helen Buchholz. *Courtesy of Laura Stellhorn*

First Presbyterian Church in Sandusky on Jackson and Washington streets, circa 1925. The church was built in 1854. *Courtesy of William H. Grahl*

Marquette Club Halloween party, circa 1920. Amelia Bing is sixth from the left in the third row; Ferd J. Bing is third from the left in the last row. *Courtesy of Amelia Davlin*

The fountain in Washington Park, August 1927. The "Boy with the Boot" statue had not yet been placed in the fountain. *Courtesy of William H. Grahl*

COMMUNITY

Ohio Beauty Pageant held at Cedar Point, 1927. The winner was Evlyn Wilgus of Russells Point. Beryl Starr was Miss Sandusky. *Courtesy of Sandusky Library*

Knights of Pythias with the floral mound welcoming tourists in Washington Park, 1930. *Courtesy of June Rupp*

Zion Lutheran Church confirmation class, circa 1940. Marilyn Gast is in the first row seventh from the left behind Pastors Stellhorn, Jr. and Sr., holding the book in front of her. Zion Lutheran Church was on Columbus Avenue and Jefferson Street. *Courtesy of Brenda Bahnsen*

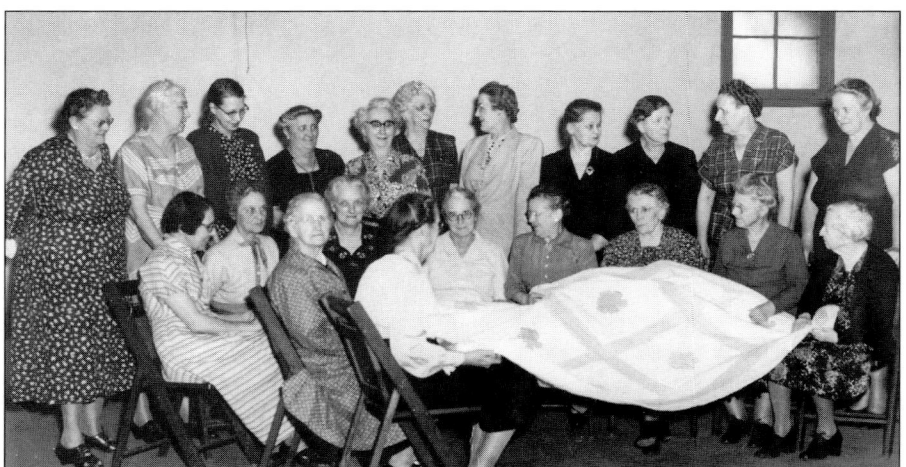

Women's Guild of Calvary Episcopal Church quilting, 1940. Hattie Gilbert is in the center. First row: Harriett Voight, Emma Gardner, _____ Voight, Emma Wilhelm, Jenny Ott, Florence Clark, Gertie Gale, Ann Petersen, Addie Montgomery, Erie Turk, Nettie Langenfelder, Mrs. Joeseph Rentz, Alt Beckley, Jane Quick, Bess Schoephle, Minnie Broom, Inzie Dean, Grace Dean, Jennie Asher, and Ruth Layton. *Courtesy of James Arthur*

For Over 125 Years We Have Been
Building the Future of Healthcare

Firelands Regional Medical Center is a 300-plus bed hospital that provides general medical services and many specialty services not usually found in a mid-sized community, to a six-county area in north central Ohio.

In 2004, Firelands Regional Medical Center began a construction project to ease parking constraints, to expand capacity for increasing admissions and outpatient visits, and to focus concerns on one of the top health issues in Erie County, the prevention and treatment of Cancer.

A 600-space free parking garage has been completed and construction of a new 85 bed patient tower has begun. The medical center's new Firelands Professional Center I, which houses the new Cancer Center and physician offices is also completed.

Visit the Medical Center's website, www.firelands.com, for regular updates about the progress of the construction.

FIRELANDS
Regional Medical Center

Sandusky

*There for you then...
Here for you now.*

Over 120 Years of Service.